You're Worth Fighting 4
BLOOD, SWEAT & TEARS

SHUNTELL ALSTON

DEDICATION

This book is dedicated to anyone battling cancer or other life obstacles that seem impossible and you want to give up. This story is meant to inspire, encourage, and motivate you to keep going and keep pushing no matter what. Even when you have to stand alone and fight for yourself when nobody else is, always remember that battle is still worth fighting and you are still worth fighting for.

CONTENTS

ACKNOWLEDGMENTS

I would like to thank my readers who have stuck with me through my last two books and continue to stick with me on my journey of writing . It is my hope that you all continue to walk this journey with me as I continue in this fight of life.

1 BLOOD

As you remember I ended the first book with God showing me over and over that He was in control. Now it's February of 2012. I began to get very ill. I was at home in the bed sick from chemotherapy. It was a Monday and the following Thursday I began to start throwing up a green substance. My temperature was 103.7. I started taking Motrin to but it was not helping. I called my daughter and told her that I needed to go to the hospital. She asked me what was wrong and I told her that I was very weak and was throwing up a green substance and my fever would not break. Then I stated, "It doesn't matter what is wrong with me, I just need you to get here fast."

My daughter pulled up thirty minutes later and I felt extremely weak as I walked to the car. I took a garbage bag with me and began to throw up in that the whole ride to the hospital. We pulled up to the emergency room door. I got out of the car and was completely bent over as I walked in through the doors. There was a nurse who saw me entering and she could tell I was in a lot of pain. She noticed the bag in my hand and she called for assistance. The nurse and an assistant rushed over to me with a wheelchair. After helping me into the wheelchair, they rolled me to the back of the room. They began to work on me and put an IV in my arms and started drawing blood. The doctor walked into the room and asked me if I had someone with me. I told the doctor that my daughter was with me and was parking the car. I mentioned that my husband was overseas so my daughter had to bring me.

The doctor told me that I was very ill. I was too weak and exhausted to fully understand what was going on. I told them my mother lived in Gary, In and my father in Memphis, TN. The doctor said, well, your counts are zero and if your heart stops, do want us to resuscitate? I just looked at her with a blank stare. She asked me again, "Mrs. Alston, would you like us to resuscitate you in the event your heart stops?" I looked down at the bed and replied, "Yes, I don't want to die by myself. Can you get my husband here?" I began to cry. She responded, "We are already in the process of contacting him."

Within 48 hours my husband called the hospital. The nurses' station answered his call and informed him that I was very ill. They asked him what would he like for them to do if things take a turn for the worse. My husband told them to do all they could to save my life. He informed them he was on his way home. The nurse brought the phone to my room and placed it up to my left ear. I heard my husband's voice and he called my name. I began to cry. He said, "Bae, hang in there. I'm on my way home. You are strong and you can beat this. You better not die on me, you hear me?" I told him, "Okay." He told me to fight. He said, "We are warriors and we cannot be defeated." I replied, "I'm trying but I am so weak." He told me that he understood but to trust that we can defeat anything that comes our way. Then he said, "Please hang in there and I will call the nurse back in a little while. I am with you and I will always love you. I love you so much and I am on my way home." I said ok and told him that I loved him too.

Now, no one knew all of the pain I went through and was going through. No one knew how difficult the struggle was trying to do this all on my own because I had no other choice. I felt like my life was over and I just did not want to die alone. As the doctor continued to work on me by drawing blood and sending it off to the lab for expedited results, they began getting my room together for my admission into the hospital.

I was in the Intensive Care Unit for 5 days and was on antibiotics the entire time around the clock. My head began to hurt and the pain was excruciating. My friend, Carol Woodard came to the hospital and prayed for me. I really needed the prayer. I began to hear 'I am the light of the world. If you follow me, you won't stumble through the darkness.' That is a scripture from the Holy Bible that came from John 8:12.

I was in the hospital for two weeks with my body in pain and discomfort. I was depressed because I felt I had no one to call on. Remember earlier I mentioned that my mother lived in Gary,

Indiana. She was recovering from heart surgery so she could not come down. My dad was unable to come and be with me for my chemo as well since he lived in Memphis, Tennessee. Keep in mind that I have 8 brothers and sisters and yet, no one could be there for me. My Aunt Von called me every day while I was in the hospital and she told me not to give up and reminded me that God has the last say so.

As the days continued to pass, my counts began to rise and things started to look better. I stopped having to get the preventive blood clotting shots in my stomach. What really lifted my spirits was the fact that I was being moved from the Intensive Care Unit to a regular unit in the hospital.

After being released from the hospital, I went home and had to take it easy. I was still pretty weak due to my condition and the medicine. I was tied down to a hospital bed for 10 days with no one to talk to, but with God, I was able to carry on. One of the lessons I learned from this was, we as people need to learn how to love one another and pray for your brother and sister.

The following Tuesday of being released from the hospital, I was scheduled to go to chemotherapy. Staying positive was difficult, a constant battle. I thought to myself, 'back to the same ole thing. It's time to put this poison in my body, so let's get it over with.' There is a scripture in the Holy Bible that reads, 'And this shall be a sign unto thee from the Lord, that the Lord will do this thing that he hath spoken;" (Isaiah 38:7).

It is okay to have doubts sometimes; it happens to every Christian but what is not okay is getting comfortable with the doubt and letting it linger. Doubt does one or two things to our faith, it either motivates us to find out the truth and become sure of what we believe or it drowns out the voice of faith and causes us to become weak. See, I was becoming weak but I had to stay focused because I refused to let it destroy my life. I knew I had to fight this demon off. That's exactly how I saw it, as a demon. I decided it had done enough. The Lord had been blessing me every day of my life that He allowed me to live. He kept me here so I could tell my story. When everyone walked away, the Lord was right there with me.

2 SWEAT

Now after I went to bed, I imagined all of the food and sweets I could eat. I wanted to cook me a full course meal and just eat my heart out but I had to stop and think. I had to remind myself that I had to have surgery in the morning. I started to strategize how to pull off not even going to have the surgery. I kept trying to tell myself that I was okay and that I didn't need surgery, but my spirit was telling that I had to have the surgery and handle business. My mind was racing like the cars that compete in the Indy 500. I finally decided to close my eyes to try and get some rest. I realized that I was not able to eat and had to stick to the fast the hospital required for the surgery. I laid down under my husband and thought about just how blessed I was to have him. For once in my life, I realized that even in the midst of all of this, I was still truly blessed. As I began to fall asleep, my phone rang. My friend Shareece was calling me. She asked me what I was doing. I replied, "What can I do. I am having surgery in about six hours." She laughed and told me that I would be okay. I responded and said, "Girl, that's easy for you to say because I am the one that has to go under the knife. You aren't. You will be at home." She replied, "I am going under the knife with you." I asked her if we were really going together and told me yes. I was so relieved that my best friend was going to my surgery with me. We continued to chat a little about the good times we had in the past as we laughed. We both agreed to let each other get some rest before the big day the next day and ended our call by telling one another we loved each other.

Now the time arrived for me to go in to have surgery. My husband woke me up and I got up and began to wash my body in the sterile wash the doctor gave me to clean my body to prep for the surgery. I dressed myself and my husband and I were off to the hospital. By the time arrived to the hospital, I felt queasy and weak. As we walked in and sat in the waiting area, I kept telling my husband that I didn't want to go through with this surgery. I repeated it over and over again. He tried to comfort me by assuring me he was there with me and would still be once I came out of surgery too. I tried to make him understand that he couldn't understand how I was feeling about it and though he couldn't possibly imagine what I was going through I knew he was empathetic to my situation. I explained to him that even though he was there with me physically, I still felt alone, weak, scared. I expressed that I couldn't understand why I was battling this disease. My friend Shareece arrived and shared some encouraging words and told me that I would get through this and it would be used as a part of my testimony as God was in control and was still on the throne. I agreed with her but I also couldn't understand how that same God could allow me to be afflicted with this disease. In my mind, I am thinking and at the same time sharing that I try to help everyone and to my knowledge, I hadn't done anything to anyone that would warrant this type of hell. Shareece replied, "sometimes God uses his strongest warriors to fight the toughest battles." I said, "yeah, yeah, yeah," and we all started laughing.

The staff came and escorted us back to the room. One of them spoke and said, "Mr. Alston you're here back from Afghanistan." My husband replied, "yes I am." They were looking at him with judgment in their eyes as if they were asking themselves why would he leave to go over there and leave me here to battle cancer by myself. My husband reminded them that he sacrificed himself to go over there to make sure he could provide the health coverage and money needed to make sure I received the treatment I needed to survive. After being asked how long he was staying, he shared that he would be home for three weeks then would be deployed again but would return shortly after. In that moment I was thankful that my husband was able to be with me even if it was only for three weeks but at the same time, I felt upset because I thought life just wasn't fair. I had thoughts of committing suicide, I felt alone and like I would suffer forever. I couldn't really describe the magnitude of what I feeling and going through. As a cancer patient and like most, I didn't want to hear people telling me they understood what I was going through because they can't understand it. I just wanted someone to truly listen, hold my hand and be there for all of the 13 months I had to undergo chemotherapy and for all the surgeries I had to have. It was all so conflicting because even in the middle of all that I was feeling, I couldn't ignore that I was still blessed to have my husband home and be there with me during this time. My friend and my husband waited in the family waiting area as they took me back for surgery. The surgery was a success and now I had to focus on the rehab that was ahead of me.

It was September of 2012 and my husband began to transition into coming home for good from Afghanistan. I felt a sense of relief and like an enormous burden had been lifted off my shoulders because I would finally have my husband beside me continuously for the rest of chemotherapy and for the upcoming major surgery I was scheduled for. My husband suffered trauma too. He lost a lot of soldiers in Afghanistan. A few weeks had passed upon my husband's return and I noticed he slipped into a state of being sad and depressed. He felt the death of some of the soldiers were his fault because he thought he had let them down by not being able to save them. He wanted all of his crew to come home when he did but everyone did not make it. My husband would sit around the house in the dark listening to music and watching videos of his soldiers in Afghanistan during the time they were all together. He started to walk around the house at night with his gun. I began to become scared, not for myself, but scared for him. I could see that he was now in a state of deep depression but he did not want to admit it. He just felt like he let a lot of people down. I tried to reassure him that he didn't let them down and I told him that it was not his fault. I tried to encourage and him and began telling him he could not blame himself and continue to beat himself up. I was trying to help him win the battle with his depression while struggling to win the battle with my own depression. Even with all the sadness, anger and depression he was dealing with, he never laid a hand on me. He would just sit in the dark. I began to think to myself, 'okay I have my husband home but am I losing him;' I didn't know what to think. We cried together and prayed together. I tried to keep telling him that it's not over and you get through this. He also shared that he felt he had let me down too since he left me by myself to battle the cancer alone. I explained to him that he did not let me down because he did what needed to be done to ensure I received the best care possible so I could survive. I was still here because of health insurance, because bills were paid, because of his sacrifice. My husband was also trying to survive over in Afghanistan to continue taking care of me. He carried a lot of weight on his shoulders. Upon returning to the United States, life for him was just not the same. I don't know everything he went through, but I know he experienced a lot of trauma because he lost a lot of friends while overseas and probably witnessed some of their deaths. Though I could not understand what he went through, I could feel it. He lost some of his best friends, Perez, Nick, Medscar, and more. He was so hurt and could not bear to look at the families when he went to visit because he was consumed with guilt. Perez's mother explained to him that it was not his fault and that he needed to let it go. My husband and her had a special bond because she was his godmother. She encouraged him daily and checked in to make sure we were both doing okay. She was vital in helping me to help my husband get through what he was going through. In the midst of all of this, there were bouts where he was still trying to be there for me and help me out too with my battle with depression and this cancer. We struggled together for so long, but we never gave up on each other and when one of us was having a better day than the other, we told the other that we would make it through this.

We decided that counseling was definitely needed if my husband was going to overcome his depression. My husband started going to counseling and after a while, his mood started to get better. We started going back to church, trusting God more and praying more. This was necessary not just for my husband, but for me too. My husband was still trying to get over the pain of losing so many people he loved and cared for. As a wife, you don't want to see your husband suffer so I started asking myself if there was something I could do to help ease his pain. He was with these men every day. They slept next to each other, fought next to each other, ate next to each other, took care of one another, and hung out together. They became family. As time went by and he continued to work through his issues, depression, and guilt with his therapist, he began to turn a corner. I was reminded that in life we have to go through some things in order to gain some things and sometimes that journey is painful.

We went through an unbelievably tumultuous and lengthy storm together. When he went overseas, I knew it would change him, but I didn't truly know what that would look like until he came back. He had to learn how to adjust to society and being home again. It took a very long time for him to adjust. He was a completely different person, but I weathered the storm with him as he did and continued to do with me. I could not give up and this storm caused me to shed tears for my husband and work hard to be for him what he had been for me. Suddenly, my battle did not seem so big because he needed me. You ask yourself what you need to do when two people need each other and you don't know where to begin. There were many nights I was on my knees crying out to God pleading with Him to help me and my husband. I asked God to give me the wisdom, tools, and resources to help my husband. I was determined that the enemy was not going to win. I was determined not to allow this storm to destroy us individually or our marriage. Believe me, this almost broke us. The enemy played a role in this storm too, but we had to be bigger, better, and stronger than his tactics and prayer was the answer for this part of the battle in this storm. I took a stand and told God, "Here I am Lord. Guide me and help me," and told the enemy he had to go and no weapon formed against us would be able to prosper.

As my household continued the battle of depression and cancer, we started moving into a place of peace as we continued to trust God. We were working our butts off to win this battle. I kept taking chemo pills after completing chemo and radiation along with having several different types of surgeries as the months and years passed while my husband and I continued our therapy. Our faith was a little stronger and we were becoming stronger and realized that we were still going to win no matter what it looked like and that it exactly what began to happen. Just when you think you are leaving the valley and heading to the mountain top, here comes the enemy with more mess and here come God with more tests of faith.

It is now December of 2017 and, in my mind, things are looking good. During one of my check-ups, the doctors found more cancer in my left breast. They told me I would need another major surgery on my breast to remove the cancer. Remember, I mentioned in my first book of this series that I had to undergo this same surgery during the beginning of my fight with cancer on both breasts. It was extremely difficult for me the first time around. They also informed me that my breast implants were leaking after reading me the results of my mammogram and other scans. I would need to have reconstructive surgery again after the removal of the cancer. I began to think to myself, "Lord, you're putting me through this again?" Then I realized that this is a journey that is necessary for the testimony He will use to help save others and fulfill my purpose. I told myself it's not over yet and fighting is what I needed to continue doing. I told myself, "Shuntell, you got this!" This time, my husband was here with me. After hearing the news, the doctor left the room briefly and we prayed together. My husband turned to me and said, "This is just another obstacle and the same God that allowed you to beat it before, is the same God that will allow you to beat again; we got this." I replied, "We got this. We've been through so much and nothing can stop us because we are unstoppable." The doctor entered the room again. I asked him how soon did I need to have the surgery. He informed me that his nurse would schedule the surgery during check out and give me the instructions to prep for it before going in.

After leaving the doctor's office, my husband and I decided to go out and have a little fun. We did some shopping, went to lunch, and went home to watch movies. We decided to take things up a notch. We called some friends over and we talked, laughed, listened to music, and more. It was our own little personal party. I started to tell our friends that I was getting bigger breasts, ha ha ha ha ha. My best friend started laughing and told me that I need bigger breasts. I replied, "They're going in to cut them out so I might as well get bigger ones." My husband agreed with my best friend that I didn't need bigger breasts. We all started cracking up and made light of the situation. I thought to myself, if it's not one thing, it's another.

The day came for me to have surgery. It was January 16, 2018 and my husband and I went into the hospital at 7:00 in the morning. When I arrived and saw the doctor, I said, "Hey, put me some bigger breasts in since you keep cutting on me" and he replied, "Mrs. Alston I don't know what I'm going to do with you." Then he turned to my husband and asked him what was he going to do with me. He said I was something else. We all laughed. I spoke up again and told my doctor not to forget to give me big breasts like *Dog the Bounty Hunter's* wife. The doctor told me I could not get breasts that big due to my small back. I told him I would manage and we all burst out in laughter!

Now it was time to go into the operating room. My husband kissed my forehead and the doctor gave him a small round object that looked like a cup holder. He told my husband that the nurses would keep him updated every hour and when the device glowed red, it meant I was out of surgery. He told my husband once the surgery was complete, he would come out and inform my husband about how the procedure went and give post-surgery care instructions. The doctor and nurses surrounded me in the operating room as I lay on the table. The doctor asked me if I was ready and I told him I was ready. They administered the anesthesia and told me to count to three. Instead of counting I said, "Don't forget that I want big breasts." The doctor said, "one, two, three…. goodnight."

3 TEARS

The surgery to remove the cancer from my left breast and to reconstruct both my breasts had been completed. I spent one day in recovery in the hospital and was released to go home. The four tubes that were placed in me for post-surgery care remained. My husband had to drain them each time they were full. As the days and weeks went by, my body began to heal but it was painful. I was in a lot of pain. I made sure to take the pain medication I was prescribed to help me through my recovery. After so many weeks, it was time to go back to the doctor for a post-surgery check-up. The doctor decided the tubes could be removed since I was healing well. I thanked God for keeping me through all of this and for allowing me to see another day.

After a couple of months, I returned to work. My husband and I returned to our normal daily routine and life seemed like it was good and we had conquered the worst of our storm. Then in May of 2019 during one of my doctor visits and tests, I was diagnosed with Lupus. My tears of sorrow that turned into tears of joy were not transforming back into tears of sorrow. I could not believe it. I had beat ovarian cancer and was in the beginning stages of remission of breast cancer after countless surgeries and having both breasts removed. I just started crying.

When I arrived at home, I was an emotional wreck. I walked into the house and told my husband that I was just diagnosed with Lupus. Shortly after that doctor's visit, I was scheduled to go in for more testing. They ran a lot of tests. The nurses and doctors kept telling me how sorry they were about me having to go through this because they understood that I had already been through so much. I shook my head and thought to myself, 'the Lord must really give the toughest battles to his strongest soldiers' because I really going through it. This nightmare seemed like it would never end. I was put on a treatment regimen for the Lupus and just continued to press forward.

As the months passed, my condition began to stabilize again, but I started having a new symptom in my left shoulder and arm. In January of 2021, I was informed that I needed to have another surgery. I was in a lot of pain and didn't understand why. When I went to the doctor to see about the pain in my shoulder, I was told I had a torn rotator cuff. I was scheduled to have surgery to fix it in April of 2021. Out of all the surgeries I had up until this point, I would have to say that surgery was the most painful of them all. I cried and cried and cried because I was in so much pain. I was off work from April to July and during my recovery and my arm did not seem to be healing very well. It was still painful and I could not raise my arm above a certain level. During my last check up before going back to work, the doctor told me I needed to come back in for another surgery to break up the scar tissue that was hindering my arm from healing properly and to fix a screw that had come out of place so, my doctor extended my leave of absence. You can imagine the pain I was in for months. The doctor assured me that once he fixed those issues, my pain would subside and my arm would heal properly. So, I agreed to have the surgery. The doctor performed the surgery in the Summer of 2021 and this time I could tell the difference. The pain was getting better and I was making progress in therapy. I was so happy this challenge was coming to an end. Throughout this whole time, I pushed through and continued working on my events for my foundation because there were people still counting on me.

I pushed through the pain, fear, disappointment, sickness, and bouts of depression because God never gave up on me. He never left me. After all that I have endured and am still enduring, I still have to tell God thank you because I know there is still someone out there that has it worse than me. I had to remind myself that God is still with me no matter what I am going through. He knew exactly what I was going to go through before it even happened and He had already made provisions for it all. I prayed for God to heal me, bless me, and make me new. When I look at my life, I realize that in all of this adversity, God has truly made me over. He has shaped me into a better person. He snatched out everything that was old and not like Him and replaced it with new life, new joy, new perspective, new faith, and new peace.

To those who feel like life has caused you to enter into a place of no return please allow my story to encourage you and be an example that there is no such thing as too hard when you take it to God and when you decide that you are worth fighting for. Everything in life happens for a reason. The enemy will even step in during a season of testing too to try to get you to waiver, doubt, and be paralyzed with fear. Sometimes he may even attack from all sides. Every time something attacked my body and God allowed me to beat it, here come the enemy with something else saying no you are not free. Everything the enemy said I could not and would not have, do, or be, God said yes. Yes, I can, yes, I will, and yes, I am. In the midst of all of this, I am growing my organization and taking care of my grandchildren. I am starting to realize that I am stronger than I thought. God told me that He was preparing me to go out and spread the news about who He is and what He can do. Every test in my life has been turned into a testimony and every test that turned my emotional and mental state into a mess has been turned into a message. It is my job now to encourage people to keep fighting and to never give up. It is my job to let them know there is a God. If He never allowed me to be sick, I would not know Him as a healer. If He never allowed me to be depressed or suicidal, I would not know him as a mind regulator. If He never allowed me to question how I would make it through and doubt, I would not know Him as a way maker. I cannot testify what I have not been tested on and I cannot encourage and inspire without the necessary tools and lessons that could only be gained from my experience. I spent 14 days in ICU and the doctors told my husband that I was not going to make it, BUT GOD! There is a God and all you have to do open up your mouth and talk to him. Pray. He will answer. His will for my life was not what I wanted. His answer was no sometimes, but His will is always best. He may not come when you want Him but He is always right on time.

I do not need another surgery. My cancer is in remission and now I am crying tears of joy because God saved my life. My husband and I are doing well and I am continuing the journey of walking in my purpose.

Let me leave you with this… always remember to put God first in your life no matter what you are going through. He is always there. Trust in Him even when you cannot trace Him and most of all, never forget to fight on because YOU ARE WORTH FIGHTING 4!

ABOUT THE AUTHOR

Shuntell Alston is an author, radio show host, cancer and suicide prevention advocate, military wife, mother, and the founder of a nonprofit organization, *You're Worth Fighting 4*. Shuntell is a two-time cancer survivor. She has fought Ovarian and Breast Cancer and was recently diagnosed with Lupus. She has dedicated her life to empowering those who feel like giving up when life has reached the peak of the impossible in addition to advocating for and supporting cancer patients and their families concerning treatment, medication, and more. As she continues her own fight in the ring of life, she is a shining example of what it means to never give up.

ABOUT THE ORGANIZATION

You're Worth Fighting 4 is a nonprofit organization created to provide moral and financial support to cancer patients and their families to lighten the load of medical and prescription costs. It was founded in 2016 by two-time cancer survivor, Shuntell Alston. After surviving her own battles with cancer and experiencing the challenges of having to go through it alone while watching others do the same, she decided that something had to be done to help support the patients and their families. She could not help but notice there were so many different types of cancer, but only one major type of cancer was continuously the topic of conversation, breast cancer. Though it is definitely more common, she knew that all cancer patients deserved the same access to resources and support. You're Worth Fighting 4 became the beacon of hope and advocate for ALL CANCERS because they all matter.